W9-ATX-668

TELEVISION
and
RADIO

Troll Associates

TELEVISION and RADIO

by Louis Sabin

Illustrated by Joseph Veno

Troll Associates

Library of Congress Cataloging in Publication Data

Sabin, Louis.
    Television and radio.

    Summary: Describes the development of radio and
television and the effect of instant communication on
our daily lives.
    1. Television—Juvenile literature. 2. Radio—
Juvenile literature. [1. Television. 2. Radio]
I. Veno, Joseph, ill. II. Title.
TK6640.S23   1985   621.388   84-8446
ISBN 0-8167-0310-8 (lib. bdg.)
ISBN 0-8167-0311-6 (pbk.)

We live in a world of instant communication. Through radio and television, we can listen to a speech being made in a country on the other side of the world. We can watch astronauts step onto the moon at the very second it is happening. We can pick up a telephone and have a conversation with someone living nearby or thousands of miles away.

Telegraph and teletype machines flash messages to receiving stations anywhere on Earth. We use these forms of telecommunications all the time. They are everyday tools in our modern world. Yet not one of them existed one hundred fifty years ago.

Communication, itself, is not new. Animals have always communicated by sounds, such as barks, whistles, clicks, buzzes, and roars. And they can communicate by moving their eyes, heads, tails, and other parts of their bodies. Human beings also use sounds and motions to communicate. But human beings can do something no other animal can do— communicate complicated ideas, thoughts, and feelings.

People can tell a long, involved story about something that happened in the past. And one person can tell others how to build a house, throw a ball, do a dance, play the piano, and millions of other things. All of these are pieces of information we communicate to each other.

Human beings have always communicated with one another. But until modern times, their communication was limited in time and space. The only ways to relay messages over long distances were to write a letter and send it, or to give the message to someone who would carry it to its destination. These forms of communication were very slow.

For example, the American Declaration of Independence was signed on July 4, 1776. Yet the news did not reach England until sometime in August of that year. Today, a declaration of war or independence is known everywhere immediately after it happens.

The first giant step in instant communication was taken by the American, Samuel F. B. Morse, with the invention of the telegraph. In 1844, Morse tapped out the message, "What hath God wrought?" on a telegraph key. This signal was carried on a telegraph line between Washington, D.C. and Baltimore, Maryland.

Less than twenty years after that first telegraph message, telegraph lines were linking many parts of the nation. The Civil War, which was waged from 1861 through 1865, was the first war in history to be reported by electrical means. Communiques from the battlefields and lists of casualties were telegraphed north, east, south, and west. Communication had entered the modern age.

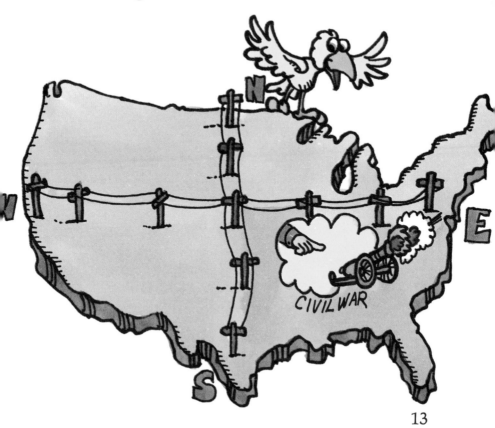

By the beginning of the twentieth century, telegraph cables had been laid beneath the Atlantic Ocean. They connected North America with Europe. This made possible the first transoceanic communication. In addition, the telephone, which was developed by Alexander Graham Bell in 1876, was in fairly common use throughout North America and Europe.

Telegraph and telephone systems depended on wires to carry their electrical signals. Where it was impossible to place wires, telegraph and telephone service was not available. Furthermore, wires could be affected by bad weather, accidents, and other problems. The invention that allowed instant communication without the use of wires was the radio.

In 1895, an Italian, Guglielmo Marconi, the inventor of the radio, first sent signals similar to Morse code by radio waves. Other scientists improved on Marconi's prototype. And in the early years of the twentieth century, it became possible to send voice signals by radio waves.

Radio broadcasting, as we know it, began in November 1920. Station KDKA, in Pittsburgh, Pennsylvania, broadcast the news that Warren Harding had been elected President of the United States. There weren't many radio receivers at that time, so only a small number of people heard the announcement. Within a few years, however, there were a great many radio stations with regularly scheduled programs and a widespread listening audience.

Today, millions and millions of people listen to words and music on the radio every minute of the day. We have car radios, miniature transistorized radios, short-wave radios, citizen's-band radios, clock radios, radios that plug into electrical outlets, radios that run on batteries, and radios in planes, boats, submarines, and spacecraft.

No matter how simple or complex, and no matter how large or small they are, all radios work on the same principle. When a sound is made into a microphone, it is turned into electrical energy. This energy, in the form of radio waves, spreads in all directions from its source. In a way, it is like water ripples expanding in circles from a place where a pebble has struck the surface.

Radio waves are invisible and electro-magnetic. They travel at the speed of about 186,000 miles per second. That is also the speed of light, another form of electro-magnetic wave.

Radio waves travel through the air around the Earth. These waves surround us all the time, in the form of tiny vibrations. But we can hear the vibrations only through a radio receiver. This receiver picks up radio currents in the air. The current is electrically amplified, or enlarged. It is then converted back into sound by a speaker. When this happens, we hear the same sound that was originally made into the microphone.

Even though the radio waves, or signals, from many radio stations are in the air around us, we do not hear them all at the same time. That is because radio stations broadcast at different frequencies. A frequency is the number of times radio waves vibrate in one second.

When you turn on your radio and place the dial at a specific number, you are setting it at the frequency used by the station you want to hear. For example, if the number you dial reads 92, you'll hear a radio signal broadcast at 920 kilocycles, or 920,000 cycles per second.

Even before radio became commonplace in the modern world, scientists and engineers were working to develop a system to transmit pictures as well as sound. By the late 1930s, television was almost ready to take its place beside radio. However, World War II interrupted its development. So, it wasn't until the late 1940s that commercial television broadcasting began.

The growth of television was even more rapid than that of radio. At first, there were just a few programs on a few local TV channels, received on bulky, black-and-white sets.

Within a short time, technology and public demand made television a twenty-four-hour, multi-channel form of information and entertainment. The invention of the transistor and the introduction of color created sharper, even more true-to-life images.

Today, in the United States, there are as many television sets as there are people. And these sets receive signals from a number of different sources. There are regular open-circuit TV stations and networks; closed-circuit TV systems, used for security and special transmissions; cable TV systems, for which a subscriber pays; and public television stations supported by voluntary contributions.

Space exploration opened up a whole new area of telecommunications. In 1962, a communications satellite, called Telstar I, was placed in orbit above our planet. It was the first sending and receiving station for radio and television signals.

Satellites such as Telstar pick up radio and television signals, amplify or strengthen them ten billion times, and relay them back to Earth. Since the first communications satellite was sent up, many others have followed. They have brought enormous changes in worldwide telecommunications.

In 1865, when President Abraham Lincoln was assassinated, it took twelve days for the news to reach England. Today, we can watch a live telecast of a royal wedding taking place in Europe or the Olympic games being played anywhere on Earth. Communications satellites also make it possible for people to dial telephones directly to many locations in the world.

Communications satellites have many uses. Weather forecasting has become far more accurate and reliable because of the data transmitted by satellite.

Mapping the world's geography has become more precise, based on the pictures and data from satellites.

In addition, the fishing industry uses satellite readings of the ocean to determine areas where ships will find a high density of sea life. In a world whose population continues to expand, this could prove to be an important tool in the battle against hunger.

Our world is shaped by communication in countless ways. And as telecommunication continues to improve, the world will, in a sense, grow ever smaller. If an earthquake occurs in Peru or Italy or the Middle East, people in distant lands know it instantly and can send aid within hours. When a scientific breakthrough occurs anywhere on Earth, the facts are broadcast, by sight and sound, to scientists around the planet. This can improve the quality of life for everyone.

Clearly, telecommunications are among the most important, influential forces of the modern world.

Comer sano

La carne y las proteínas

Nancy Dickmann

Heinemann Library
Chicago, Illinois

www.heinemannraintree.com
Visit our website to find out more information about Heinemann-Raintree books.

To order:
☎ Phone 888-454-2279
💻 Visit www.heinemannraintree.com to browse our catalog and order online.

Edited by Siân Smith, Nancy Dickmann, and Rebecca Rissman
Designed by Joanna Hinton-Malivoire
Picture research by Elizabeth Alexander
Production by Victoria Fitzgerald
Originated by Capstone Global Library Ltd
Printed in the United States of America in Stevens Point, Wisconsin.
Translation into Spanish by DoubleOPublishing Services

062011
006257RP

Library of Congress Cataloging-in-Publication Data
Dickmann, Nancy.
  [Meat and protein. Spanish.]
  La carne y las proteínas / Nancy Dickmann.
    p. cm.—(Comer sano)
  Includes bibliographical references and index.
  ISBN 978-1-4329-5130-6 (hc)—ISBN 978-1-4329-5137-5 (pb)
1. Meat—Juvenile literature. 2. Proteins in human nutrition—Juvenile literature. I. Title.
  QP144.M43D5318 2011
  612.3'98—dc22   2010027736

Acknowledgements
We would like to thank the following for permission to reproduce photographs: © Capstone Publishers pp.**5**, **12**, **14**, **22** (Karon Dubke); Corbis p.**13** (© Image Source); Getty Images pp.**4** (Kevin Summers/Photographer's Choice), **10** (Inga Spence/Visuals Unlimited), **11** (Dorling Kindersley), **21** (Jon Feingersh/Iconica); iStockphoto pp.**8** (© Ronald Fernandez), **23 top** (© Mark Hatfield); Photolibrary pp.**7** (Jo Whitworth/Garden Picture Library), **9** (Animals Animals/Robert Maier), **20** (Peter Mason/Cultura); Shutterstock pp.**6** (© BESTWEB), **15**, **23 middle** (© Juriah Mosin), **16** (© a9photo), **17**, **23 bottom** (© Joe Gough), **18** (© Monkey Business Images); USDA Center for Nutrition Policy and Promotion p.**19**.

Front cover photograph of meat, fish, eggs, nuts, and beans reproduced with permission of © Capstone Publishers (Karon Dubke). Back cover photograph reproduced with permission of iStockphoto (© Ronald Fernandez).

We would like to thank Dr Sarah Schenker for her invaluable help in the preparation of this book.

Every effort has been made to contact copyright holders of material reproduced in this book. Any omissions will be rectified in subsequent printings if notice is given to the publishers.

Contenido

Carne, pescado, huevos, frijoles y nueces

La carne y los frijoles son alimentos que comemos.

4

También comemos pescado, huevos
y nueces.

La carne proviene de animales como las vacas.

Los frijoles provienen de las plantas.

atún

El pescado proviene de animales como el atún.

Los huevos provienen de aves como
las gallinas.

Las nueces crecen en los árboles.

Comer estos alimentos puede
mantenernos sanos.

Ayudar a tu cuerpo

La carne, el pescado, los huevos, los frijoles y las nueces contienen proteínas.

Necesitas proteínas para crecer.

Comer frijoles te da energía.

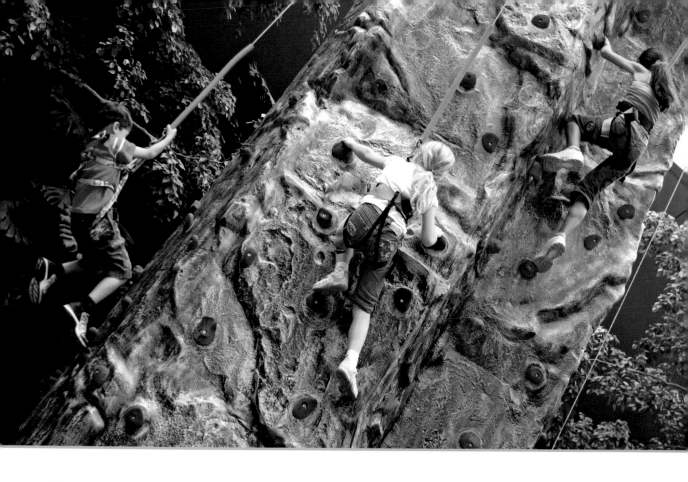

Se necesita energía para trabajar
y jugar.

Comer carne y pescado es bueno
para la sangre.

Algunas carnes tienen mucha grasa.
Demasiada grasa es mala para
tu cuerpo.

Comer sano

Debemos comer diferentes alimentos todos los días.

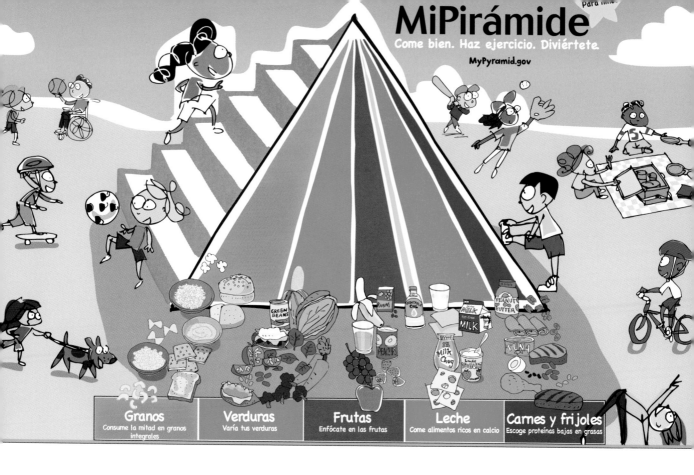

La pirámide alimentaria indica que debemos comer alimentos de cada grupo de alimentos.

Comemos carne y otros alimentos ricos en proteínas para mantenernos sanos.

¡Comemos estos alimentos porque
son deliciosos!

Busca la carne

Ésta es una cena saludable.

¿Puedes encontrar la carne?

Respuesta en la página 24

Glosario ilustrado

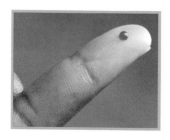 **sangre** líquido rojo que está dentro del cuerpo. La sangre lleva alimento y aire a todas las partes del cuerpo.

 **energía** capacidad de hacer algo. Necesitamos energía cuando trabajamos o jugamos.

 **grasa** cosa aceitosa. La grasa mantiene el cuerpo caliente. Es malo comer mucha grasa.

Índice

Respuesta de la prueba de la página 22: La carne es el pollo.

Nota a los padres y maestros

Antes de leer

Explique que debemos comer una variedad de alimentos para mantenernos sanos. Presente el grupo alimentario de la carne y los frijoles. Nuestros cuerpos usan las proteínas de la carne y de los frijoles para desarrollar muchas de sus partes, como la piel, el cabello, los músculos, los huesos y la sangre. Las proteínas ayudan a nuestros cuerpos a crecer.

Después de leer

- Comente el hecho de que algunas personas no comen carne ni pescado (vegetarianos) y que otras no comen carne, pescado, huevos ni lácteos (veganos). Piensen en otros alimentos que pueden comer para asegurarse de obtener suficientes proteínas.

- Explique que algunas personas, debido a sus creencias religiosas, no comen ciertos tipos de carnes o solamente comen carne que haya sido preparada de cierta manera. Los budistas no comen carne ni pescado; los hindúes no comen carne de vaca; los judíos comen carne kosher y no comen carne de cerdo ni mariscos; los musulmanes comen carne halal y no comen carne de cerdo; los sijs no comen carne de cerdo ni de vaca. Comente experiencias de este tipo con toda la clase.